Following our Fathers:
Two Journeys among Mountains

Following our Fathers:
Two Journeys among Mountains

Linda Cracknell

best foot books

First published in 2012 by
best foot books,
Aberfeldy, Scotland

ISBN: 978-0-9562453-2-8

Cover photo, drawings and
maps by the author

Design and layout by
Mark Blackadder

Printed by Short Run Press

For my Uncle,
Martin Cracknell

Contents

Pre-amble

'Go out and stretch your legs', my mother used to say to us as children when four walls squeezed in to make us tetchy; 'get some fresh air'. It might only have taken me to the bottom of the garden then, but when I was seven, my mother 'accidentally' took me, my older brother and sister, to the top of Snowdon. She'd only intended us to walk a short distance up the path, but my brother started to cry every time she tried to turn us around. I remember the blizzards that flushed my nose into a continuous stream, and a trail of Rolos left on cairns, luring us to the summit. The idea was to descend by train, but we found it wasn't running because of snowdrifts.

As the youngest, I was always the one screaming 'wait for me' from several yards behind on family walks. I was the *'Cry Baby Bunting'* whose *'Daddy's gone a-hunting'*. However, that first mountain experience gave me the determination needed for Snowdonian peaks on school Adventure Weeks, and eventually led to a persistent longing for the hills, for the thrill of seeing a landscape open out and become comprehensible below my feet.

My twenties and thirties were punctuated by

mountaineering trips and some fairly cowardly rock-climbing, but I particularly started to enjoy long-distance walking in parts of north-west Scotland most remote from roads – Knoydart, and Fisherfield – wild-camping for five or six days with a sense of journey. I enjoyed the landscape unrolling, the rhythm and motion, the growing fitness, even the slight sense of hardship and rationed food. Only taking what you can carry generates the ultimate sense of independence. As Robert Louis Stevenson said of his crossing of the Cévennes in 1878: '… the great affair is to move; to feel the needs and hitches of life a little more nearly; to get down off this feather bed of civilisation, and to find the globe granite underfoot and strewn with cutting flints'. For me, those journeys were about climbing out of the trivia and pressure of everyday life, escaping the largely human world for a shift of scale.

In my forties, with the axe-man of fifty stalking towards me, my adventures on foot seemed to have reduced. Of course, I was still walking. Without a daily 'stretch of the legs', my body and mind feel dull and under-used; walking is an essential cadence underpinning my creativity. But I was too far within my comfort zone.

The first walk I've written about here, following a friend's father on a journey of life or death through Norwegian mountains, set my feet off in a new direction. I became less intent on 'getting away from it all', and more interested in walking paths which beat with a human resonance. The two stories in this volume are part of an exploration, on foot and in writing, of this new preoccupation – following people, stories, ancient ways, human structures in the land. I now walk as a way of celebrating both landscape *and* humanity.

More specifically, the Norwegian walk made me realise the need for the second journey in this book, connecting walking and memory. I strongly suspected that I'd inherited from my father my inability to spend a whole day indoors, especially if the sun was shining. I found that the time had come to explore *his* mountains.

Losing my footing,
finding my feet again

I take off my new walking boots and leave them with others at the door of Selma Moldsvor's house at Isfjorden. The village sits at the far end of one of the fingers of sea that penetrate deep inland between Alesund and Molde. From the window of the sun-washed living room, the Romsdal Alps are sparring high into a July sky, the light dancing off rock and the determined, late-lying patches of snow. The hills tremble with promise.

Our group of five is absorbed into a gathering of crag-faced elderly men – once climbers – and journalists. Ellie, the eldest of the Sømme siblings, chats with them in Norwegian about what I assume to be plans for our walk. My old friend Yuli, and her brother Bertie hover on the edges of this, their grasp of the language slighter because they were very young when the family left Norway in 1962. Ellie's twenty-three year-old son Oliver and I are like children, not comprehending what will happen next.

The five of us are expecting to start walking from Selma's house, but the hours talking rather than walking are creeping us into the afternoon. The focus of our trip so far has been on meeting people rather than the practical details of the journey. I have little idea of the daily distances planned, or the amount of food we need to carry before reaching the next shop. I try to bury my frustration, wait for the moment when I can breathe the mountain air and get my arms and legs swinging. I want to put my boots back on.

I met Yuli in 1982, at a spinning and weaving gathering in Devon where we both then lived. She was wearing one of those traditional Norwegian cardigans – snow-flake patterned, with pewter clasps. I was drawn to her calmness and slightly foreign-seeming beauty, and her passion for working with wool which I was learning about at the time. We became friends, later sharing a house and working in the same woollen museum. Then I moved to Scotland in 1990 and we saw each other rarely.

I had always known about her Norwegian father, who, like mine, died when she was very young. I'd seen the Norwegian flag displayed on the wall of her mother's house. The hand-written caption beneath it read: 'Flag carried by Sven Sømme when he escaped from the Germans in June 1944'.

In 2004, sixty years later, his family decided to set off in his footsteps. Well in advance Yuli invited me to accompany them – we'd finally be able to spend time together and I could contribute my experience of long-distance walking. She sent me a series of seven photo-copied maps, and Sven's own account of his journey which was produced in the 1970s as a small book, *Biologist* *on the Run**. She'd translated his route from words into a line of green ink that traversed each map. In places, the line was broken, and question marks interrupted the certainty. On the back of Map One she had written a note to say that one section of the map was missing, and she wrote an encouragement: 'I can't help saying it but I *do* hope you can come'.

For a reason I couldn't put my finger on, I remained uncommitted to joining the party as the Sømmes made their plans and got themselves fit. Perhaps it was just my own lack of connection to the story. Despite the lines and contours and place-names in black and white, the landscape remained entirely mysterious and intangible to me. It was the first expedition I'd considered since separating from a long-term partner with whom I took many multi-day walks. I didn't feel confident. I was lured by the idea of being outdoors, the mountains, the new experience that Norway would give me, but tugged back by a need for home, comfort, the steady revolution of familiar, easy paths.

In the end, about ten days before departure, I gave in to the former impulse, and decided to go with them.

The first few days in Norway unmoored me from my everyday world, while I waited for our walk to start. We

---

* Re-issued in 2005 as *Another Man's Shoes*, ISBN: 09549137-3-6

travelled through landscapes half-Scottish and familiar, half strange, growing more spectacular as the train climbed from Oslo north-west through castellated pinnacles where trolls are said to lurk, down to the towns which crouch on convoluted coastlines amidst a complex jigsaw of sea, island and mountain.

As a broadcaster herself, Ellie's advance publicity had been highly effective in alerting the Norwegian media and brought forward many people who had been involved in Sven's escape. As a result, we were met by several interested parties. We visited the fisheries college on the island of Gossen where Sven was Principal. Convinced the Allies would invade the west coast of Norway, the Germans considered the island strategically important, and it was cleared of its inhabitants for an airfield. At the island's war museum, seated around a long table decorated with candles and lupins, we were offered fish soup, *smørbrød* (open sandwiches), and countless cups of tea. Our hosts, white-haired, tanned people with little English, had beautiful faces enlivened by a memory they had to share with us.

Outside, the west coast evening stretched long and late with its layering of blue-island silhouettes reminding me of the Summer Isles.

Diminutive Selma Moldsvor stands before us in slacks and

a white blouse, keeping us indoors with stories of war-time resistance, and singing in her tremulous 80-year-old voice. After breathy attempts at composure, her speech stutters and stops. She picks up a brown paper package and holds it out to Ellie who slips off the paper, turns with a gasp to her brother and sister.

'Pappa's shoes!' she says.

A murmur scuttles around the room and Selma's face crumples between a broad smile and tears as Ellie hugs her. A sob rocks up in my own chest; some undercurrent of loss and memory ambushing me. It's deep, and inarticulate. I'm ashamed at my former impatience.

The brown leather shoes are passed from hand to hand around the room. Their laces are knotted, the tongues lolling inside, and the leather cracked, lifting from its stitching. A hole has been forced through at the left big toe, as if that foot was larger, or perhaps lengthened by a dropped arch. 'Admiral' is spelt out on a sole worn glass-smooth, holes bubbling in V-shapes at the pressure points of ball and heel. They have been well-worn – the shoes of a practical man. Shoes he was wearing when a German sergeant told him, 'You will be shot as a spy'.

Sven Sømme – 'Pappa' – has walked into the room.

Sven was active in the resistance movement. He organised intelligence, gleaning news from the BBC by illegal radio

and circulating it to the coastal communities near his island home on Gossen.

'Were not these summer days of 1944 among the greatest days of the history of the world?' he wrote. 'When four-fifths of all peoples were united in fighting Hitlerism in order to secure the human rights of mankind? Would it ever happen again that all nations would unite like this, acting like one people against one mutual foe?'

Arrested for taking photographs of a torpedo station, he was on a ship at Åndalsnes ready to be taken to military headquarters at Dombås for summary trial, when he slipped away from a sleeping Hungarian guard who had shown him considerable kindness, and disappeared into the hills with a loaf of bread under his arm.

From Åndalsnes, he skirted high land to the south of Isfjorden, dropping down again into the Erstad Valley. He aimed to find a way south-east through the mountains to the valley of Eikesdal from where he had already planned an escape route across the Dovre mountains and into neutral Sweden. Unsure of the way from the Erstad valley, he was helped by a small group of local people, including André, a young man of nineteen. Meanwhile the Germans were searching every house in Åndalsnes and had sent out soldiers and bloodhounds in all directions.

'You cannot cross the mountains in these shoes,' André said. 'Try my boots to see if they fit'.

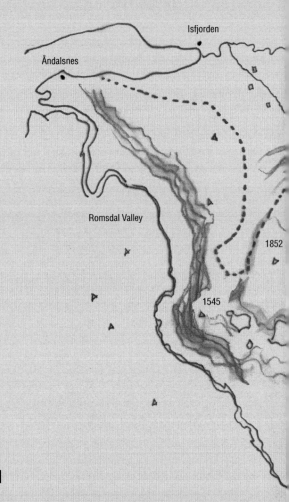

Isfjorden

Åndalsnes

Romsdal Valley

1852

1545

North

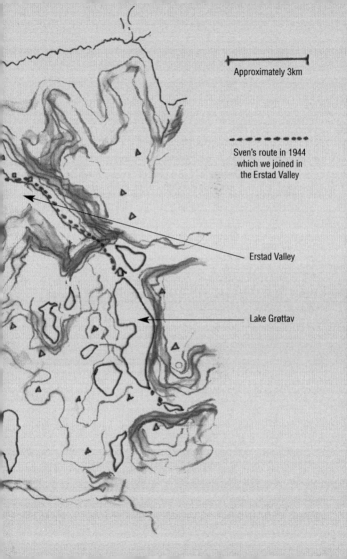

Approximately 3km

Sven's route in 1944
which we joined in
the Erstad Valley

Erstad Valley

Lake Grøttav

Leather had all but disappeared during the Nazi occupation of Norway between 1940 and 45, and people wore paper shoes with wooden soles. Nevertheless, André offered up his brand new boots. And so Sven Sømme left his shoes behind. André later became Selma's brother-in-law, and the shoes passed into her hands. They were lovingly cared for, even rescued during a fire which destroyed her home ten years before our visit.

André's gift of boots and his guidance over the mountains to Eikesdal with two other competent climbers were the initial link in a generous chain that ushered Sven Sømme 200 kilometres through wild and isolated mountain country still snow-covered in June 1944. Travelling often under cover of night without a map, adequate clothing or food, he slept in the open or in deserted summer farms, and hid frequently for extended periods before he could continue safely. Valley and mountain, valley and mountain; helping hand to helping hand. This was the rhythm of his journey. He was aware of the personal risk his helpers took, reflecting the 'morale and true friendship between men that had not been destroyed by the German occupation'.

Sven's description of the initial climb up the Erstad precipice wasn't confident: 'No path could be seen any more, but from olden times people had found their way up here to the vast mountain ranges, shooting reindeer there and carrying meat and skins down the precipice to their farms in the valley below… We had to cross several small glaciers which were hanging on the mountainside. I did it with the feeling that any moment I might rush 1,200 feet to the bottom of the ravine…'

Sven's guides secreted him into the folds and corries of the terrain, and gave him a window-frame to carry so that if challenged he could claim to be going to work on a mountain hut.

When the party reached the top of the precipice and a plateau – a frozen landscape of mountain, lake and river – the lower valleys looked to him, 'like deep and narrow cuts made with an enormous knife'. They passed a hut beside a lake which was buried by snow, right over the chimney. He was travelling only a month earlier in the year than us, but that winter had seen momentous falls. Nevertheless, he felt safer once high in the mountains: 'No German soldier had ever set foot up here, nor was he likely ever to do so… The mountains were ours'.

The mountain story Selma has told, traversing both danger and safety, has fortified me for the journey. So does her home-made pea soup, flat-bread and cheese. Standing in the garden as we make our final preparations, she strokes my bare shoulder and chats to Ellie. I sense in her touch the assurance that what we are about to do is important.

Photos are taken, journalists' notebooks filled, and we repack luggage so that items we won't need for a night in a mountain hut can be transported by road to Eikesdal. I still know little of the plan but Sven's account of 'the precipice', and a dense band of contours I've seen on the map, have given me some concern about how we'll cope with the climb. A lean, tanned, grey-haired man with startling blue eyes keeps glancing at his watch and frowning at our delay. Then he's introduced as Oddmund Unhjem, our volunteer mountain guide for the first two days of the walk, and I immediately feel less worried.

Oddmund leads us up a shaley rock-strewn path under looming crags. We start to get the measure of our own fitness. Oliver, 6′5″ and a ski instructor, lopes along comfortably. This is his first mountain adventure on foot, and his conversation is studded with exclamations of 'cool' and 'wicked'. Having lived and walked in Scotland for fourteen years, I'm surprised when he points to one of a succession of cairns, and says, 'Do you think these piles of stones are deliberately put here, to show the way?' He farts his way up the steep slope, laughing, exhilarated by the sound of his body working.

An arthritic knee keeps brother Bertie hobbling slightly at the back, but Oddmund allows us frequent stops. He tells us he's 73 years old, but it's hard to believe. We all breathe more heavily than he does.

Mist awaits us above, hanging and billowing in the cleft of the precipice. A river throws itself down in a mighty waterfall, just as Sven described. Oddmund finds for us the hidden windings of the path between the crags. The story starts to come alive. And we take delight in finally using our bodies to retell it.

We climb out of the valley, and reach the plateau at 1,000 metres after only two and a half hours. The air is cool. Peaks and pinnacles tower over the turquoise waters of Gröttavatnet. We make ourselves at home in the hut which was buried under snow when Sven passed sixty years earlier, and we cook up couscous and noodles.

The summer evening avoids nightfall like a child on holiday, a mist colluding with the sunset to drape the mountains with rose-pink blankets. A couple are celebrating their thirtieth wedding anniversary with a night in the hut. The light evening extends for so long that another couple who have joined them for a meal don't leave the hut until 10pm to walk back down to the valley.

Sven and the companions who guided the first part of his journey shouted, sang and called to each other as they walked across the plateau:

'Is this the right way to Stockholm?'

'Right, O, just turn left at the second set of traffic lights.'

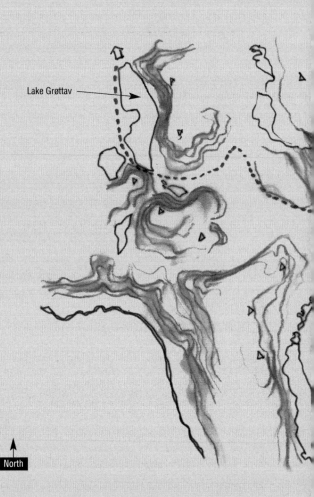

Lake Grøttav

North

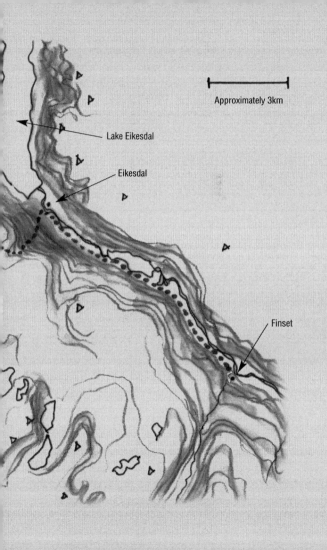

He was clearly exhilarated, not just by the conviviality of the group, but by the scenery. He wrote about the view at the end of the plateau, just before the drop to Eikesdal, where 300 metre waterfalls dangled. Each side of the lake was, 'flanked by wild mountain scenery... The mountains grey and blue with greenish-white glaciers like collars around their necks...'

'I realised now,' he concluded, 'that it would have been madness to try to cross the mountain alone... First the Erstad precipice, then twenty-five miles across an unfamiliar mountain landscape, and then how would I have been able to find my way down the Eikesdal?'

They dropped down the steep side of the valley and then walked ten kilometres up to its head at Finset. The farmer, Nikolai Finset – whose Father, Kristian, Sven had met 24 years earlier – sheltered Sven in his house. Nikolai's ten-year old son, also named Kristian, was sworn to secrecy.

It's a bright, cloudless day when we leave the hut, clattering steeply down to the shores of Gröttavatnet through loose boulders, and 'skiing' on our boot soles where remaining snow allows. Bertie stumbles, slowed by his painful knee. As we wait for him, Oddmund expresses concern about our pace, considering the distance we still have to go that day, and about how Bertie will cope with

the steep descent into Eikesdal. We each take some of the
weight from his rucksack.

At the southern tip of the lake, we pick up the rough
road which crosses a high plain of rock and shimmering
snow. It's a long, hot stomp. Bertie's knee swells further.
He limps. We wait. When an all-terrain vehicle chugs into
sight about halfway across, he takes the offer of a lift. The
rest of his time in Norway will be spent in the valleys.
Close to the road where we wave him goodbye, a rotten
timber frame has been cast aside, partially buried in long
grass and we claim it as a physical remnant of Sven's story
– the window-frame he carried as a disguise.

Finally we stand on the eastern edge of the plateau, just as Sven had done, looking down at Lake Eikesdal snaking a narrow mirror away from us between sheer slopes. This wild mountain country, this glorying in the heights, is what I've come for. My desk and computer seem remote and irrelevant.

We descend 1,000 metres, zig-zagging down the wall of rock through steep birch forest, wading through flowers, grabbing at blueberries as we pass, with sheep bells clanking around us, down to the green flat meadows and farms of the Eikesdal valley: a deep low groove cut into a high land.

We're met by Kristian Finset, the Kristian who as a boy had kept quiet about the man hiding in the spare bedroom. We're expecting to camp, but he offers us beds in his house. Kristian is a quiet man with a kind, round face. Following a stroke four years earlier, he's only gradually recovered his power of speech and doesn't know the place of things in his kitchen. His wife died from cancer just one month earlier, but his face broadens into a grin each time one of his grandchildren appear. Under his shirt cuffs, I notice the edge of a cream-coloured wool interlocked vest, the sort I wore at primary school and have never thought of since.

The next morning we are tourists – showering under the tallest waterfall in Europe, swimming in the lake, discovering *potatokake*. Our biggest worry is how to keep the chocolate from melting. Then we walk slowly up the valley towards Finset where Kristian's son, another Nikolai, gives us accommodation at the family farm. The walls inside the clapper-board house are cluttered with photographs of weddings, and a framed needlepoint for each new child, stitched by their grandmothers. Kristian shows us the room where his father had concealed Sven.

That evening we walk up into the blunt end of the valley to visit Kristian's daughter, Marit, in a turf-roofed timber house she and her husband have built. We sit in a garden backed by a sheer cliff. Her eighteen-month-old son powers across the lawn on all fours while the other children are scattered to the hills to fish or pick flowers amidst the same buildings and bridges that watched Sven pass.

Marit tells us about her job as a high-powered IT consultant, working from home. This arrangement seems to highlight the difference between rural life in Scotland and Norway. Human history and contemporary presence meet in this landscape – even the places most remote from urban influence may be inhabited. In Scotland such places are more often abandoned, remaining haunted by a sense of previous presence.

Below Nikolai's farmhouse the water sprinkler pulses and the river rushes all through the night. I watch dawn from the deck, looking back through interleaving slopes of the valley walls. They define, where they meet, the way we've come. The V of sky to the north-west never darkens. A thin mist settles in a kink of this valley that invisibly links members of the Finset family – Kristian, Nikolai, Marit – in a line of homesteads now gently ticking with sleep.

Sleepless myself, I imagine the Sømme family as a kind of valley that stretches back in time with parents, grandparents, stories, photos. It stretches ahead too, with children; cousins who become keen swimmers and ski instructors. And the valley intersects with others in this landscape of my insomniac creation; other family valleys with legacies running backwards and forwards through it in seams, connecting through the story of Sven's escape.

I observe the genetic legacy of the family who follow Sven, noting sulkily how as I am now 45, there will be no-one in the future to walk after me. Looking the other way, into their past, tickles up something like envy. Sven's children have found a way of bringing their father closer, memorialising him in a walk, and it's been made possible because a memory has been so vitally kept alive.

'If I ever grow up, shoot me,' Sven had apparently instructed his family. I wonder if my own father might have said something similar. I have no memory of him. He died of cancer in 1961, just as Sven did. Although he was a keen mountaineer, I know little of what and where he climbed. I have no scent or record of his adventures. For all I know, he might even have climbed here in Norway.

My own valley seems strangely punctuated. I'm inclined to think of myself as a full stop.

Before he left the Eikesdal valley, Sven copied a very rough map of his route onto a piece of sandwich paper. Nikolai supplied him with oats, butter, bread, pork, dried milk, a towel, soap, thread and a needle. Then he gave Sven a rucksack to carry it all in, and accompanied him out of the valley, up towards the elevated Lake Aursjøen.

Nikolai carried three heavy planks on his shoulder. It only became clear what these were for when they reached a narrow canyon down which a stream writhed. He laid them across the rocks from one side to the other to make a bridge. Sven's hands were seized in farewell, he crossed, and the planks were removed. He was alone with no retreat.

Sven worked his way along the lake-side, wading some of the streams and rivers cascading with melted snow, until he reached an unoccupied *seter* – or summer farm – at Gåsbue, where he slept the night. At the next *seter* a young man chopping logs told him that there had been Germans in the area, searching for a man escaped from Åndalsnes. A little later, he saw two men on the

Finset

North

Approximately 3km

Our route

Lake Aursjøen

Gåsbue

Dombås

hillside, observing the area with field glasses. After that he walked by night.

He had passed the watershed dividing the east and west of Norway but now attempted a difficult crossing of a major and swollen river, getting drenched and cold, and having to retreat to avoid swimming. He had made it his habit to walk for two hours, lying down to sleep, then walking again to avoid hypothermia. Finally, walking upstream, he found a bridge over the river, and then he crossed the railway and main road between Oslo and Trondheim. Hares and their shadows were making a playground of the traffic-less night road.

The military headquarters at Dombås, where he would have been taken for trial, were to his west, and further Nazi installations to his east. But now he could look ahead to the Dovre and Rondane mountains and to arriving at his friends' at Lake Atnsjøen, which he estimated to be a further 80 kilometres.

Even now that he had the rucksack, he deliberately carried little, wanting to cover ground quickly. 'My principle was to carry just enough to survive and as light a burden as possible so as to be able to cover a great distance in a minimum amount of time.'

We've each bought a new rucksack for the trip and put too much into it. Ellie, Yuli and Oliver unload some unnecessary things to send home before we leave the farm at Finset. Kristian weighs each pack on his farm scales. Mine is heaviest at 18kg. It includes my own tent and stove, the trappings of independence in case I should leave the party and go off alone. It's an indication, I think, of my wavering commitment to the project when I set out. Now we no longer have assistance transporting our luggage, my hips and lower back begin their argument with the weight.

It's another of Kristian's sons, Viggo Finset, who accompanies us on the steep climb out of the valley. With sun smouldering on our shoulders and young birch flaring up the silver-grey rock, we climb until we can look down onto the roof of the farmhouse. The flat-bottomed, steep-walled Eikesdal valley stretches away, impossibly green. The river finds its wooded edges, first on one side, then the other, meandering in a pleasing line towards the Lake.

Viggo needs no planks to set us on our way. The stream runs dry since a hydro-electric project diverted it. But two generations on, the geography of Sven's escape still runs deep.

As we take the old path beyond the crossing point, scratching through juniper, blueberry and young birch towards a dam, I enjoy the sense of walking a storyline; a line that began for us with Sven's shoes. The goodwill offered to our own journey in memory of the original one seems remarkable. Although it's a story to which I thought I had no connection, I feel uplifted and claimed by it.

At the dam on Lake Aursjøen, Viggo leaves us to return to the farm. We are not able to follow Sven's route along the shores of the Lake because it has since been flooded for the hydro. Instead, we are pushed higher onto a bleak moorland. We strike out for our first unassisted night, finding small patches of turf between the boulders on which to pitch our tents as dusk falls at ten-thirty.

Despite the great kindness of all our helpers and guides over the last days, I feel some excitement when we reduce to four – Ellie, Yuli, young Oliver and myself – and become truly independent. Now we will feel Stevenson's 'cutting flints' more keenly.

We close in around the campfire, eating chocolate-covered marzipan and comparing blisters. With charac-teristic ingenuity, Yuli has protected her toes on the walk with small curls of fleece she brought from home. The effect of pressure and moisture has felted the wool into tiny socks, fashioned to the precise mould of her own toes. She's created artefacts of surprising beauty which we all admire.

When I first knew Yuli she was spinning and weaving, but more recently she's started to make felt, creating colourful and gorgeously textured fabrics which form

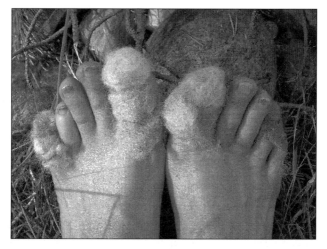

hats, coats, wall hangings and even shrouds for green burials. Our creative lives have developed in parallel, both of us driven by them, seemingly unable to escape their demands. One of us creates fabric; one text. I like the idea that our crafts are linked by an ancient metaphor. The capturing of stories onto written paper invoked the word 'textus' from Medieval Latin, meaning 'thing woven'.

We read aloud from Sven's book in the firelight and I think of the note Yuli wrote to me on the back of Map One, which we have now walked beyond. She said of her father's book: 'Do hope you enjoy it and get inspired. He (Sven-Pappa) was very much a man of his time. He was a hunter but after he fell in love with my Mum he became more of a shooter with the camera – my Mum's influence!' Yuli had wanted me to like him.

His words act as a touchstone now, a reminder of what was at stake, and they reinforce the meaning of our own walk. Because in some senses we are walking for pleasure, it's easy to forget how it would feel to be here alone, and in danger. We have good boots and equipment, no Nazis in pursuit, no need to travel in the night.

Despite his discomfort and fear, joy frequently surfaces in his account, buoying him with a sense of tremendous freedom: 'I had escaped torture, imprisonment and death, I was free like the birds singing around me. There was no school any more, no more responsibility, no property to take care of. Life was ahead of me. I was an outlaw.'

Sven's love of the mountains, his holidays spent skiing, swimming, fishing and hunting, had given him a thorough knowledge of the land. To reach the high passes without leaving a scent that hounds might trace, he waded up burns. In order not to leave tracks across patches of snow, he bent the tops of supple young trees down to the ground and then used the resulting 180 degree 'flick' as a means of pole-vaulting to the other side.

His love of his country, its people and its nature clearly sustained him. He heard a Scottish accent in the

scolding rattle of the ptarmigan: 'rack-gack-gack-garrr'. His spirits rose as he watched a herd of reindeer gallop through a bog, becoming lost in the spray of water and moss that rose from their hooves.

We enjoy reading of experiences we've shared with him already: red squirrels trapezing through branches; golden plovers making their plaintive call, 'tleee', and running fitfully towards us. Like him we've grazed on blueberries and wood sorrel in the forests. In marshy areas, we've picked cloudberries whose taste Sven characterised as 'sunshine'.

I sleep better in the familiarity of my tent. Rain patters on the fly sheet in the night, but when I get up in the morning, it's dry and the clouds are parting. I wash myself in the small pool we're camped beside. Every time we pass such places, Oliver asks enthusiastically, 'Do you think there are fish in there?' But I meet none. We brew coffee and prepare ourselves for the day's walk towards Dombås, unsure how far we'll get.

The path crosses a featureless plateau, and circles behind a small hill, after which we descend back towards the Lake through rocky outcrops and the welcome embrace of young, green birch. We spread out, each falling into the step of our own world. There are views along the 20 kilometre length of the Lake, and we arrive at a cluster of tourist cabins at Gåsbue where we meet a small road, and therefore, people. We cook up tea and some vege-burger mix, and realise how tired we are. Not much further along the lakeside road, we make our next camping stop amidst a band of carnivorous mosquitoes.

Oliver wakes up the next morning disenchanted with the journey – he has been bitten all over and is starving. The remaining rations are low, and are very unappealing to him. After we set off, he walks a long way ahead of us. When we reach a campsite where we hope to find a shop, it's closed. We tough out a long, hot stretch of road from the end of Lake Aursjøen towards Dombås discussing our food fantasies. Chicken, lemon curd, apple juice and roast potatoes are Ellie's. Yuli, Ellie and myself blast out an African greeting song to sustain our steps, and Oliver hides his head in embarrassment when a group of cyclists approach.

The second campsite has no shop. Depression begins to brood around us. It's still over 10 kilometres to Dombås. Just when we most need cheering, a couple in a camper van give us juice-rich apples. When they offer us a lift to Dombås, we take it.

Soon we are eating pizza and cake in a café and watching people go by, noting the temperature climbing to 34 degrees now that we are sunk in a valley and on tarmac. I prod at the sore spots ground into muscles around my pelvis by the weight of my pack.

Oliver, demoralised, and with other priorities, decides to leave us here and go home despite wanting to support his mother and honour his grandfather on this journey. We all feel the loss of his youthful energy, but it's hardest for Ellie as we wave him off from the railway station the next morning. I wonder how it will feel now to be three. We award ourselves a rest day and spread out the remaining maps for a planning session.

I have with me a small metal map-measuring wheel. It's the only one of my possessions I believe to have originally belonged to my father. We run it along the lines made by Sven Sømme's feet, measuring the distance. I enjoy using the wheel for this but am also pricked by something like sadness. As if the feeling is locked under ice or seen through smoke, I'm not quite able to identify it.

I show Yuli and Ellie how to estimate the time each section of the walk will take with the slowing effect of ascent taken into account. We research the location of shops to replenish food stocks, and decide on a stopping place for every night. The map becomes less abstract; the journey is now constructed in our imaginations to its end.

After the freezing river and the speeding hares, Sven found a valley to follow south-east into the Dovre hills, hoping that it would lead to a mountain pass and over to the Grimsdal valley. It was difficult in the dark, traversing

a series of steep ravines slippery with frozen snow. He found himself at 1,500 metres above sea level, following a line of cairns that poked through snow and mist across an endless-seeming plain.

On this bleak, high crossing, he sank into an emotional crevasse. He saw a pair of lapwings – the male sitting on a stone and the female running between boulders – noted that they were far from their usual coastal area, but felt nothing. 'My heart was numb', he wrote. Marching hour after hour along the cairns he thought of his family and friends, the Germans, his narrow escape, and could provoke no strong response. He worried: 'Would that feeling last after I had returned to normal life?'

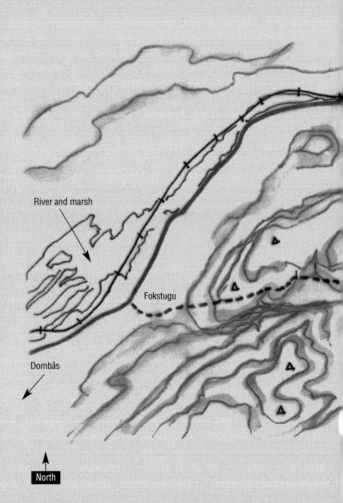

River and marsh

Fokstugu

Dombås

North

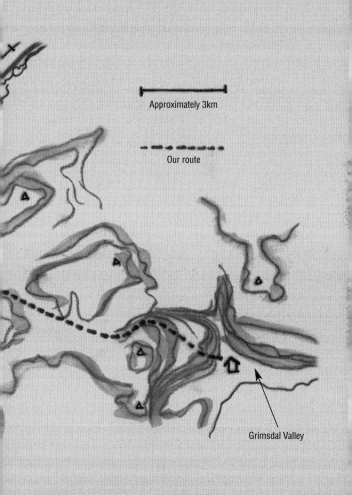

Approximately 3km

Our route

Grimsdal Valley

But the landscape lifted him again as he began a gentle descent, down amongst birch woods, juniper, open meadows. Finally he could see a rough road winding beside a shallow river which ran to the south-east, and the Rondane Peaks rising beyond. Below him was a group of *seters*, a tourist hut, cows and goats grazing.

'There was no doubt that this was the Grimsdal valley. I had arrived where I was hoping to be'.

A short taxi ride out of Dombås rejoins us to Sven's route just after his river crossing. We walk from Fokstugu across the Dovre hills, climbing steadily onto a plateau bleakly reminiscent of the Cairngorms. Grey shale has been shunted about by thousand-year-old glaciers and speckled with yellow lichen. It rains.

Ellie looks about and shivers. 'He was so exposed,' she says. 'Imagine how invisible a grey Nazi uniform would be here; how easily a small figure moving alone could be picked off by a sniper.'

But when we look closely, we find the grey desert mocked by miniature 'gardens' – cushions of bright pink moss campion, fluorescent green mosses, and alpine anemones, Sven's favourite flower.

'They belong to the mountains,' he wrote, 'where in early spring the first snowless patches appear. They peep up from the ground, pudgy buds, clad in a fur coat of grey,

silken hair… They are the flowers of freedom.'

He was confident the German soldiers would never see this flower, or him, so anxious were they to stick to what they called 'civilisation'.

On a shaley hill, climbing out of the last dry glaciated river bed in the Dovre hills, I stumble. I pitch forward down the slope. And at some point, hands out, realise I am going right down, not recovering my feet. My shin strikes something. Then 18kg of rucksack follows gravity, hits the back of my head and cracks my face onto rocks.

'You look pale': a voice.

I put on a fleece.

'Your nose is crooked,' says Yuli.

Blood drips from somewhere. My forehead. Shaking and shock.

There are one and a half hours still to go to the Grimsdal hut. I find a compacted lump of last winter's snow, and walk with it pressed to my forehead.

During the walk, the arrival at the hut, the tent going up, the attempts to emulate normality by eating waffles, cream and strawberry jam in the hut's cafe, purple fluid swells into bags at the corners of my eyes. My brow feels top-heavy.

'I'll be fine if I rest,' I tell the others, thinking of our plan for the days ahead; afraid of my first ever night in a hospital.

But Yuli shakes her head. 'I really think you should have it seen to.' A friend of hers had a head injury when they were on a cycling holiday together, and she is all too aware of the dangers.

My new boots are scuffed and sun-worn, and we are about half way along the route to Sweden. I've walked for six days, just got my rhythm, finally got on good terms with my pack.

Tears come for the second time in the trip as Yuli and Ellie smile sadly, waving me off in a taxi to rumble down the track to the nearest village doctor. I look back at the V-shaped groove which has beckoned for the next day, the entrance to the Rondane range, regarded as the finest alpine hiking country in Norway and an inspiration to many Norwegian writers. I am not sure whether I'll be back.

Rather than treating me and returning me to Yuli and Ellie as I hoped, the doctor dispatches me into the night. I travel south in another taxi to Gjøvik and hospital, with a driver nodding at the wheel after his full day at work as a butcher. We aquaplane on mountain roads transformed to rivers by a sudden storm, lightning filling the 2 a.m. sky. He has travelled the world, he tells me, as Norway's number one boogie-woogie dancer, but now would like to be a rally-driver, to experience the thrill of sliding, almost losing control. I fight sleep during the three hours our journey takes and try to keep him talking.

Perhaps aware of my fears, he sees me into the hospital. A woman gives me a pair of pyjamas and a bed, and looks after me as if I'm the hospital's only patient.

'We try our best', she says.

She wakes me in the morning, asking, 'Did you manage to sleep at all?'

I feel my way into all the sore places I hadn't noticed before – stiffness in my left arm, a cut under my watch-strap.

But when I see the consultant he tells me that my

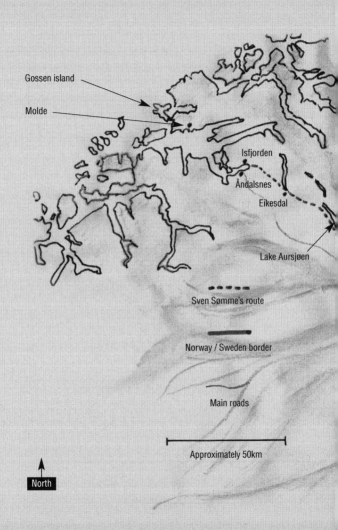

Gossen island

Molde

Isfjorden

Åndalsnes

Eikesdal

Lake Aursjøen

Sven Sømme's route

Norway / Sweden border

Main roads

Approximately 50km

North

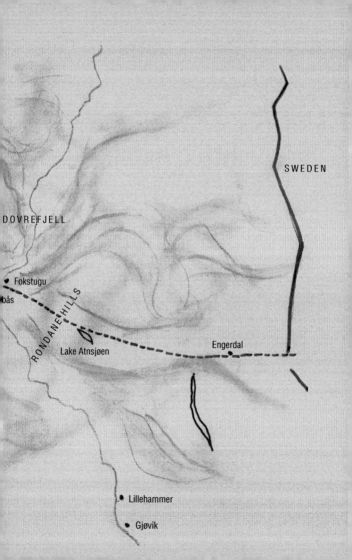

nose is too swollen to be treated now; I have to fly home.

By 9.30 a.m. I'm discharged, an Elephant Woman straining to see the world beyond my own face because of the swelling across the bridge of my nose.

Then I'm walking alone around Lillehammer; in an internet café booking an early flight home; waiting for a bus. A woman and her child look at my bruises in momentary horror. When the woman makes eyes contact, she looks away. The child does not. I see other people reacting in such ways. Perhaps it seems that I've invited a beating.

The reminder of the biting hills rises all around me as I travel back up the country to retrieve my belongings. I am in Peer Gynt country; I am following an ancient pilgrim's route that should be calling my feet; I am hazed and estranged. I sleep in a motel below Grimsdal, dream of my mother, waking at each revisit of the fall with my hands fluttering out to save me.

The motel manager knocks on my door in the morning.

'No headaches?' he asks, seemingly pleased that I'm still alive.

I find a telephone box, pump in coins on a call to my sister to tell her what's happened. Standing on the brink of self pity and tears, I fight to stay on its landward side.

Although many people turn away from the trouble

they seem to read in my face, it's strangers who help me with arrangements for my pack to be brought down from the mountains. A check-out girl in the supermarket near my motel picks up the telephone to the hut warden. Her father arrives smiling with it at the supermarket.

Then I turn south again. As I arrive off the bus in Oslo at midnight, a prostitute outside a nightclub is the only person who stares directly into my face and asks, 'Have you had an accident?' It's as if we share an underworld.

I leave Oslo on an early morning flight.

Thankfully, Sven did better than I did.

Not long after Grimsdal where I left the route, he arrived at Nesset, a farm he knew well, belonging to the Norwegian Academy of Science. His friend Hjalmar and sister Inga who lived there didn't recognise him at first in his lean and ragged state, but helped him to hide out for several weeks in a tent above Lake Atnsjøen, while waiting for the safest moment to head for Sweden. From here he managed to make contact with his wife, saw his brother Knud, fished, watched otters and divers, and was treated to food and rest while he re-planned a route and enlisted the help of friends to cross some major rivers to his east. Along with a false passport and ration cards, he received a message written in invisible ink. People of his home district of Romsdal were overjoyed that he'd out-witted the nine hundred German soldiers sent to recapture him.

Then he pressed on east, travelling through dense forest, crossing rivers and lakes and increasingly marshy land, making contact as he did so with the helpers pre-arranged by his brother. Sven met a man late one night, and they stopped to chat 'as wanderers used to do when they met in the mountains'. He knew to trust the man when he offered him a cigarette.

'I see you are the right person', the man said, finding that a piece of paper inside the packet matched his own. He then led Sven to the river.

The most dangerous part of his journey ended with a knock on the door of a Swedish farm-house, 'the door into freedom'. He became one of over 48,000 Norwegians who walked or sailed to safety.

After Sweden, he came to Britain in September 1944 to join the Norwegian Ministry of Agriculture, returning to liberated Norway in 1945 in King Haakon's convoy escorted by the British Navy. He gave each of his helpers a watch engraved 'in grateful thanks for your help in 1944'. They are still shown off by descendants today.

In the days following my fall, I pictured Yuli and Ellie, the remaining journeyers, small figures in a high, wide landscape. They were well-equipped, confident and deter-mined. Although I was sorry not to be with them, I was

proud to have been part of their journey. Like Sven, they rested up at Nesset. They found their father's signature in the visitor's book and met Hjalmar's widow. Then they pressed on through wolf and bear country, the bogs and rivers, to finish just short of the border into Sweden two and a half weeks after setting out.

Their steps had reinforced their father's route, but they had also worn their own pathways of personal meaning. For Ellie it was a way of experiencing a little of the effort the journey had cost him, and a means of reclaiming Norway as a country to which she belonged. For Yuli it was a kind of route-finding towards her father. But it was also political, a response to a new climate of war following the invasion of Iraq the previous year.

Reaching their final campsite at Engerdal, they lit eight candles for the river to carry. There was one for each of us who'd set out on the current journey, one each for their mother and father, and one for the Hungarian guard on the ship at Åndalsnes who they learnt was shot for the

carelessness which allowed Sven to escape, and saved his life.

As dusk fell, they watched eight small lights float down the river in remembrance of a man whose funeral in 1961 they did not attend. Then in celebration of a journey, they ceremoniously burnt the socks that had both cushioned their feet and chafed up blisters.

Sven's story remains marked with its own memory-stones; a white-pebbled path visible in the dark. Like the best folk tale or legend it has been passed on, and then on

again. Sven may have avoided leaving prints in the snow for his trackers to find, but he left lasting markers in people's minds and in their concept of the landscape.

I set out on this walk principally for a holiday, but it came to mean much more. I discovered a richly peopled landscape. Even the strangeness of the days following my accident, with generous strangers playing their part, contributed to a sense of a living, resonant pathway.

I returned home thinking about this. I wanted to follow more whispering ways; to seek out stories that still echo underfoot. And I began to wonder if that could include a faint path with a strong personal connection.

I started asking questions, and I acquired a photo. Summer 1952 in the Swiss Alps. A young man, slim and fit, stands with hands on hips in front of a pine tree. He has a cravat around his neck and a face that, although shaded by a squint-brimmed hat, hints at features like my own. He died only eight and a half years after he looked so alive here with his hemp rope, canvas rucksack, rolled up shirt sleeves, wearing a grin. I began to wonder if I could identify one of his journeys, or even a route he had ambitions for, and walk a memorial to him.

But I had doubts. It might mean a climbing expedition in the Alps – something formidable that I had never done – and I no longer trusted my own feet.

Outlasting our Tracks

A single electronic note by my ear stands me upright at 3.45 a.m. I tiptoe towards the others in their dark bunks, and Colin raises a hand. I understand immediately that he's been awake for hours – in the last ten days the three of us have named ourselves the 'Insomniac Mountaineering Society'. But Rick's shoulder needs a shake, a whisper to pull him from a dream.

Rick had greeted the previous morning sardonically: 'I didn't expect to see spindrift on my summer holidays'. Mutinous winds and blizzards blasted us over the Grünhornlücke pass towards the Finsteraarhorn Hut. Through huge windows we then watched cloud-shadows dance along the summits of the white range opposite. The conditions had sent us to bed questioning the viability of today's climb.

A glance through the window now reveals a miracle: Stars. A skyful of them. Colin has told us the rule his father had in the Alps – if you can see five stars, you go for it. There's no discussion. Rick brings to the breakfast table the news that not only is the sky clear but the wind has stilled. There's a sense of a charmed day emerging. The other climbers at the hut, few enough because of the bad weather the preceding days, are as alert to the promise as we are.

Alpine huts before dawn are brutal places. The air of the crowded boot room thickens with the sound of zip-pulling, plastic rustling, the thud of heavy boots on wooden boards, the clunk of ice axes. Climbing harnesses jangle with metal hardware as they're strapped tight. Our efficiency is tripped up by apprehension, things not to forget, lack of space. No-one makes eye contact.

By 4.45 a.m. we're jolting our bodies into life by scrambling up the steep rocks behind the hut. The blue and white markers painted amongst the shelves and chimneys that make up our path, lurch up late in the head-torch beams. My lungs feel pinched by 3,000 metres of altitude and by my pack pressing from behind. As ever it's heavier than it should be.

Above a crest of rock we meet the ruins of the old hut and take a ridge northwards. At the boundary between rock and snow our silhouettes congregate with those of ten Italians going for the same summit. They are hard-muscled, fit-looking and a lot younger than us (collectively 150 years).

A cry goes up from Rick as first sun pricks pink the Fiescherhorn and Grünhorn peaks. During the minutes in which we put on crampons and rope up for the snow-field ahead, an illuminated pink curtain drops down the snow-covered mountain wall opposite towards a murky chasm. Later in the morning, it will bleach to white and stretch down in jaggy fingers, prising aside the dark walls of the valley to flood the Fiescher glacier with sunlight.

The ritual of roping up has become familiar over the last week and is oddly comforting now. I find the rope's mid-point and fix it with a clove hitch onto the karabiner on the loop of my harness. Then I coil spare rope tightly over my left shoulder, and tie it off to my harness in a knot. After the fumblings and uncertainties of the previous week when we were acclimatising and practising all this on climbs in the Arolla area, the tying of the knot is now almost automatic. Finally I wind a prussic loop between the rope that will run ahead of me and the karabiner. This will be vital if I fall into a crevasse.

A line of shared responsibility now snakes between us, demanding to be watched so that our distances can be adjusted for different conditions – slack or taut, depending. The rope makes a team of us, pulling us out of individual reveries and slow waking with the need to communicate. Like riding a tandem, pauses will need negotiation.

We move off slowly, no head torches needed now. Colin leads, finding a line towards a rib of rock that descends from the summit. It's high above us, but we'll level with it at a place known as the *Frühstückplatz* or 'breakfast place'. I follow, always between the other two, taking least responsibility. Between Colin's mumbling and Rick's deafness, my role sometimes seems to be to shout messages fore and aft – 'Crevasse ahead!' or 'Happy with the pace?' or 'Should we be going higher?'

By covering the footprints of climbers in the days before us, the new snow has made pioneers of us, erasing the accepted route, forcing us to be slow. It disguises crevasses and snow bridges, laying itself in soft piles that our first laborious steps sink into and compress. Those behind us will harden it into an easier-going trail. We would prefer not to be leading.

It's here on the first snow slope, as we take a line that puts us ahead of the Italian group, that my mind spools away for a few minutes, to focus somewhere inside myself. As if it's a revelation, comes the thought: 'I'm climbing the Finsteraarhorn'.

Finsteraarhorn arches its back north-south through the Bernese Oberland. The *Canton's* highest mountain had been summoning Rick and Colin for many years, and they had finally chosen it to celebrate their fiftieth birthdays in 2008, twenty five years after they first climbed together in the Alps. By coincidence, this mountain still chimed faintly in the memories kept alive by my family.

After the Sømme walk in Norway, I had asked questions about my father's mountaineering. I wanted to colour in the shaded outline in his photograph, to have some stories to walk or tell. It must have been from him that I inherited the 'mountain gene', but how little else I seemed to know.

When I asked for specifics of mountains or routes, it was only Finsteraarhorn that could still be named. My mother pointed at its daunting profile in a brown leather album. A fine sheer fin rose up. Massive ramps of rock piled one on the next to make up its western slopes. My

sister shivered when she looked at it. At half my age, in 1952, my father led his own expedition here.

If I was to answer the call to follow him, I reasoned to myself, I had to start my Alpine climbing career before I reached fifty. I thought at first it would mean joining a commercial expedition, something I always resist. But when I talked about it to Rick – an old friend who I've walked and skied with in Scotland – he and Colin agreed to absorb me into their trip, bravely, considering my inexperience in the Alps.

I sought out books, looked up the position and the terrain on Google Earth, and then opened the 1:25,000 map which bears the mountain's name. It's the only sheet in 247 of the Swiss Survey series on which not a single surfaced road is marked. A tiny area of green appears in the top left hand corner where the land drops down towards Lauterbrunnen.

I put the map flat on the floor, but it refused to lay low. Grey hatched ridges were linked by tight contours, conjuring high, wrinkled, remote land. Pale blue glaciers coursed across it, five of them radiating out from a central point named 'Konkordiaplatz' after the busy Paris interchange of Place de la Concorde. Another glacier system writhed its way up the right hand side of the paper, towards Finsteraarhorn. But Konkordiaplatz, resembling a huge ice-hydra, spread its arms as if forcing the mountains apart, to occupy the majority, the centre, of the map.

My father's party must have reached Konkordiaplatz by climbing out of the long green valley of Lötschental. My sister and I holidayed there in 2003, wading through flowers on the valley sides below the snow-sealed peaks. We gazed at the steep and coruscated glacier below the

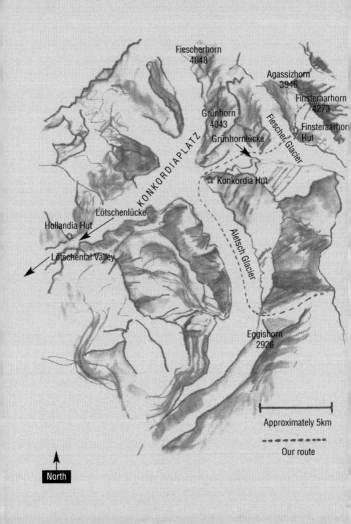

Lötschenlucke pass with the relief of those who know they're not called to it. In fact I'm sure we believed it to close the valley in rather than provide a route beyond. We had no idea then of our family connection to the valley.

A wrinkle in geography and time had Rick and his family staying in a village just up-valley from us. Colin joined him the following week, just after the death of his own father with whom he'd climbed, skied, scrambled all over these mountains. It's almost as if we were unknowingly then staking the ground for this trip.

Gaining height clarifies geography and has always been one of my reasons for mountaineering. You link up what have seemed like separate, dead-end valleys in patterns which have little relationship to what you understand when travelling by road or rail. I sensed the spars of our journeys – my father's, Colin and Rick's, my sister's and my own – spreading from that meeting place of deep ice.

Studying the map tickled up in me a sense of magic, but it was magic tinged with fear. It hinted at a world quite beyond my known territory from which I might emerge enchanted, altered. Or terrorised.

To reach the Konkordiaplatz we walked up the hydra's southern arm – the Aletsch Glacier. At 23 kilometres, it's the longest in the Alps. We dropped into a steep valley just under the Eggishorn until a cliff of ice towered a shadow over us. Then we climbed a feature I have learnt to call the 'bergschrund' – the mysterious and potentially dangerous boundary between two worlds, where rock and certainty disappear under a lip of ice.

I'd seen photos of the glacier taken from the hills above – a swathe carving north-south between corridors of high peaks like a massive bubbling river, its tail flicking south-west to narrow and melt towards the Rhone. The curves of its long slow journey valley-wards are emphasised by two dark veins of medial moraine, trapped by ice pressing in from both sides. However, as we abandoned rock to climb the first splintering-loud steps onto its pitted back, starting our journey northwards along it, we could see nothing but the surface immediately around us. The massive, ancient body – its two kilometre breadth and its steady ascent towards the glacial junction of Konkordiaplatz – was concealed in dense fog.

Disorientated, I felt I was walking on a sea that had been struck still and silent at a moment of monumental swell. For the first hour my steps were diffident. The ice gleamed up a dull grey where gravel had been trapped in visible pockets. Score lines were etched across it in great arcs. Crevasses yawned, drawing my eye down into twisted interiors – sooty black, turquoise – that shelved incrementally down to inconceivable depths. The ridges

between them rose and fell; great whale-backs and miniature mountain ranges which forced diversions to find places where we could jump the crevasses. Colin was a misty sub-marine silhouette, disappearing into a distance that was impossible to judge.

This wasn't a walk of rhythm and thought, but a strict regime of care and concentration – watching for the route; avoiding the catch of a crampon on an opposite gaiter. My head was bedevilled by the squint, gargoyled grins of stalactite teeth leering out of crevasses; by the image of Frankenstein and his monster wandering fog-drunk on the ice. I was in a faded black and white movie. Where algae had coloured old snow, tinting it pink, it lay in fat slabs against the monochrome, incongruous as steaks. It was a troubled surface, holding secrets in layers and scars, and curved scratches, burping up occasional groans. It crept at its own pace that had no need to engage with the human world, or explain itself, shaping the land around it as it went.

I thought of Scotland, its familiar valleys defined long ago by creatures such as this; valleys whose shape and residues still hold the mark and memory of ice. As John Ruskin said: 'the footmark, so to speak, of a glacier is just as easily recognizable as the trail of any well-known animal,' allowing us to imagine the seas of ice which once engulfed such landscapes.

The surface was tamed in time under my crampon claws. I gained confidence, but I longed to see the dark rock-rise of the hills that defined our corridor on either side. How would we know, I wondered, in this labyrinth of fog and crevasse, wandering at the whim of the glacier's faults and blockades, when we were level with the gothic high notch of rock to our right which held the Konkordia Hut where we would sleep that night? Might we not walk right past it?

I rallied when a slight lift of the mist revealed the dark seam of the medial moraine carving before us. Then the broad lateral sweep of Konkordiaplatz dropped below the mist curtain ahead, promising, with a white glowing stripe under the far lip of fog, the rise of further glaciers, further peaks behind it.

It was then that a photo my father had taken came into my mind.

The three in the photo – Jim Parry, Effie Pendleton, and David Lawton – are blurred in black and white, paused with backs to the camera. Standing on the glacier that's carrying them in from the south-west to where their route will meet ours at the Konkordiaplatz, a hemp rope connects the three to my father, the photographer. They stare ahead, away from him. Finsteraarhorn peaks high in the furthest eastern distance and I imagine that's what they're focussing on. It's as if the glacier has stilled

the flicker of their feet on the deep snow, forcing them
to listen to its wisdom sighing beneath them, their lives a
tick-tock in its long slow voyage.

The trail after my father has been slow. As a child, I
remember searching for photographs, trying to find proof
of his existence to fill the gap of memory. In the stiff
second drawer of the dining room desk I stole glimpses,
framed and pasted into albums.

   In preparation for this trip, I wrote to The Alpine Club,
believing my father to have been a member. I ferreted in
the memories of my mother, my uncle, a former girlfriend
of my father's. A few more details emerged, and the brown
leather album revealed its trail of black and white photographs and postcards. The dark hills and skies of the Lake
District were there, the cat Bulan perched on my father's
shoulder outside my parents' first home. There were
picnics on Devon clifftops with my mother, father; *his*
mother and father. My sister as a baby. And the house and
neat-lawned garden at Earl Richard's Road, Exeter. I
remember my grandfather sending me to collect snails,
and ending their shimmering, destructive trail-making
around his borders of snap-dragons and michaelmas
daisies by dropping them into the water butt.

   The week before he crossed the Konkordiaplatz, my
father went, like us, to Arolla. He was with a party from

the Oxford University Mountaineering Club (OUMC), climbing in the ranges that spike up from Val d'Hérens. The first pages of the album hold photos of this trip. They feature young tanned men with tangled hair, holding up wooden-shafted ice axes as they pose for shots when the going is easy. Names of people and places are scribbled on the reverse side of the photos in pencil. Two or three hands argue on some of them:

'Looking south from Petit Mont Collon?'

'No. But I'm not sure what.'

'Boquetis ridge'.

'Yes. That's it I think.'

In his postcard home of 23rd July he described their first day in Arolla – 'We were up at 5.15 this morning to do the climb up to and along the ridge shown [la Petite Dent de Veisivi] … Maybe part due to altitude we thought we couldn't make it, but did and had [a] wonderful view of Matterhorn and Dent Blanche. On ice for first time tomorrow.'

When I contacted the Oxford club, they were able to help with the Arolla part of the trip. The Journal of that year contained an account – the climb of Petit Mont Collon, traverse of the Dent Sud de Bertol, a blizzard on the Pigne d'Arolla, a retreat from the summit of L'Eveque caused by unstable new snow on top of ice, a traverse of Mont Blanc de Cheilon including the Arête Jenkins, and so on. The record had Rick remarking: 'Wow, they really went for it, eh?' And I felt a prickle of pride.

'Dick' his fellow climbers called him. I've grown up without a name for him, lost as he was to me before I had much language. I imagine him as the life and soul of the party at the campsite in Arolla, and at the Hotel Collon where they drank local wine and ate *raclette* and got thick heads at a birthday celebration. I imagine him speaking French in the huts. Perhaps, with his musical ear, he was responsible for his party, 'making feeble and tuneless responses to the gay and lovely songs of a party of Swiss', as recorded in the club journal, while they basked in the sun on Tete Blanche on the last day of the club meet. As I read the joyous words of joint adventure recorded in the OUMC Journal, Richard Cracknell, the summit-hunter began to materialise.

The Club had no record of the trip to the Bernese Oberland the following week; it was clearly an informal arrangement with two other Club members. They were also joined by Effie Pendleton, another Oxford student, and the fiancée of David Lawton. Family folk memory says my father was worried by having her along, as she was less experienced and might hold them up.

The pencil scribbles helped me trace their journey – Hollandia Hut, Konkordiaplatz. There were several postcards of Finsteraarhorn with words written on the back which fill in some of the story. Photos of the spiny ridge of the Finsteraarhorn were taken from the summit of Agassizhorn, just to its north. The photos seemed to stop there and I puzzled over how the climb of Agassizhorn related to their ascent of Finsteraarhorn. Did they return to the Finsteraarhorn Hut for a night before climbing it? Or climb the entire ridge from the north, meeting our route at the Hugisattel, now just rounding out of sight above us? Is that what had made them so late in the day?

I imagined my father, in this three weeks or so of adventure before his 'grown-up' life began, feeling viscerally alive as he breathed in fine Alpine air. He was 25 years of age in 1952, and had just finished his Chemistry degree at Oxford. He would have been disappointed that his final year's research on longevity was disqualified because the source of his studies had been discredited, but he had a job to go to with ICI in Middlesbrough. He was an accomplished enough mountaineer to be leading his own party, and had been involved in the equipment tests for the first successful Everest expedition, which he and my mother would hear news of from the Lake District the following year.

His mountain photographs feature equipment made of canvas, wool and hemp. When I prepared myself by looking at a few websites about alpine climbing gear, I was quite overwhelmed by recommendations for lightweight crampons, clothing made from Windstopper, Polartec Powershield, Schoeller Dryskin Extreme, etc. I decided to make do with a 20 year-old ice axe, borrowed crampons, wool leggings under summer-weight walking trousers.

If you listen with eyes closed as rucksacks are organised the night before a climb, there are two predominant sounds – the trill of zips being pulled and the rustle of plastic bags. My father didn't have the benefit of a plastic bag when he came to the Alps. It was not long afterwards, however, that he started to work with epoxy resins which were then a whole new chemistry, and probably brought him into contact with carcinogens. His interest in longevity was a cruel irony – a terminal cancer killed him only eight and a half years later.

As we climb the pristine snow slope towards the rocky ridge that holds the Frühstückplatz, we become aware of a muffled line drawn right to left across our way. In several places it gapes open, reveals the crinkled edges of a crevasse; the nearer we get to it, the more cavernous.

'Don't like that,' says Rick of the suggestion we cross it to our left where it reaches towards a rock spur falling steeply away into the valley.

A wide snow bridge is directly ahead of us, dipping slightly between two open mouths. Aware of the tricksy appearance of this new snow, we creep towards it a few steps at a time, as if approaching a dangerous animal that might suddenly charge us. We look up at the third option – a circuitous high route to the right which arcs into a strong-looking bridge over the crevasse. Then we focus ahead, aware of the risk we're taking.

Colin coils slack rope in his hand while behind him Rick and I stand firm, ice axe picks turned outwards, ready to brace on the ground should the surface fail him. Then he's down on all fours, scuffling across the crevasse with the rope swinging and pads of snow kicking up behind him, climbing up onto safer ground. When he's upright, it's my turn.

The snow pulls and sucks at my feet, and I'm floundering with both arms and legs as I ride the back of the deep, struggling for breath. If the snow bridge gave now, I'd surrender with relief, stop fighting upwards and sink into the depths to be free of gravity, and regain my breath.

When we are all three across and able to view the yawn of the mountain below us, we signal to the Italians to take the higher, less direct route, thus condemning ourselves to be the leading party for most of the remaining climb.

Soon we're clunking crampons onto the stone rib, climbing to the ledge of the Frühstückplatz, where we do as the name suggests, eat chocolate, and gaze at the dawn-lit mountains rising to our west in peaks and spires. The Fiescher glacier slinks through its shadowy rock corridor below us, a silent turbulent river.

We don't linger long, gripped as we are in a cold west-facing dawn. We look up to the shaded snow slope steepening above a gnarly area of crevasses. This slope defines our next two hours of ascent up to the 'Hugisatell', the saddle from which the more technical part of the climb begins.

The warden at the Finsteraarhorn Hut has warned us that it's on the steep slope looming above us now that there are sometimes difficulties after a fall of snow. It could be uneven – heavily collected in some areas and thin in others. The angle, especially higher up, could spell avalanche trouble. Yesterday this suggestion had me shivering with apprehension. Today I feel differently.

It was Franz Josef Hugi, a natural scientist from Solothurn, who declared, 'The very ascent of the Finsteraarhorn… is absolutely impossible for human beings'. Admittedly he was speaking about a different route, but on August 10th 1829 with his guides from the Hasli Valley, Jakob Leuthold and Johann Währen, he explored the route we, and most other climbers, take today via the south-west flank and north-west ridge. Because he sprained his ankle, the guides were forced to leave Hugi behind a little above the 4,088 metre saddle, while they continued to make the first ascent of this monarch of mountains. The saddle was later named after Hugi.

Edward Whymper, a legendary figure of early Alpine mountaineering, was the first to climb the Matterhorn on his eighth attempt. Four were killed in the descent, leading Queen Victoria to ask if mountain climbing shouldn't be against the law. Whymper understood risk as the crux of mountaineering, and following the accident wrote a reflection which is often quoted as advice: 'Climb if you will, but remember that courage and strength are nought without prudence, and that a momentary negligence may destroy the happiness of a lifetime. Do nothing in haste; look well to each step; and from the beginning think what may be the end.'

On our relatively short journey from the Konkordia Hut the day before, I felt my resolve falter, beaten down by spindrift-sharpened winds reminiscent of the worst day on a Scottish winter hill. As we plodded towards the Grünhornlücke, Rick's cheerful voice sprang up behind me.

'There's the sun.'

Disbelieving, I looked up and saw a pale misty disc. At regular intervals, he then gauged the unveiling:

'Sun – two out of ten.'

'Sun – six out of ten, and you've got a shadow, Linda.'

'And there's Finsteraarhorn,' he said as we arrived at the col and looked ahead where the mountain should be. A wall of fog had performed on it a vanishing act.

At each step down the other side and particularly once on the snow-disguised ice platform of the Fiescher Glacier, I expected the surface to subside and plummet one of us deep inside. Each of us sank a leg into a crevasse; it was a matter of time. I began to question the taking of risks, the necessity of going higher, exposing ourselves to avalanche danger. Not for the first time, I asked why I'd imposed this ordeal upon myself. The questions that had accumulated on pre-departure sleepless nights passed again in a chain, hand over hand. *Will I be fit enough? Will I manage the knots and ropes? Will I suffer from the altitude? Will I be afraid?*

A chorus of these doubts whispered just behind me as we approached the Finsteraarhorn Hut. I was finding enough adventure and commitment in the blizzard-scoured journey to this interior without climbing any higher.

'I'm not sure I'm up to it,' I had finally said.

But now the snow slope climbing to the Hugisatell above us looks even and firm. There is no wind, and sun is promised. All is less forbidding; hope, not fear predominates; height beckons. The trudge begins.

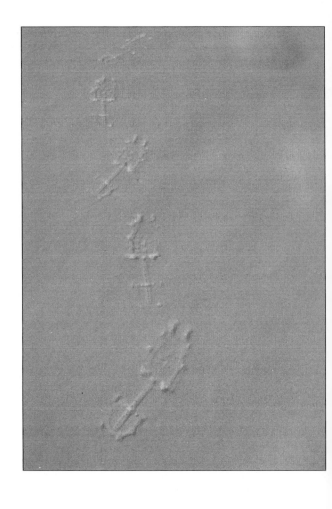

The pace is crucial. Seemingly ludicrously slow, it has to allow us to keep going for two hours without over-heating and so exhausting ourselves. Zips can be adjusted but with a harness on and roped up, clothing changes are impossible. Efficiency with time in Alpine climbing can be the difference between life and death. It's essential to descend before the surface deteriorates to slush, snow bridges weaken, banks of unstable snow succumb to gravity and avalanche. Faffing is for the Hut.

Colin, as ever, sets the perfect pace. But as ever I wish I was fitter. Although I'm never truly unfit, I've not had long days in the hills for some time, and my training at home was curtailed two weeks before departure by a fall down the stairs which cracked my ribs. I'd wondered at the time if my body was colluding with the night-whispers to sabotage my trip.

And so goes on the mesmerising trudge towards the Hugisatell, a time of breath and foot coordination, punctuated by the squeak and groan of the ice axe penetrating frozen snow. I'm charmed by the precise, crisp line of delicate claws we tattoo onto the snow, like hermit crabs' scuttled trails across white sand.

I plant the ice axe; lift my left foot through; lift my right leg through. Plant ice axe, and repeat; and repeat. Every motion is deliberate, and moon-walk slow. On slightly less steep ground, I can increase the pace by planting the axe simultaneously with one of my feet so it's a two-time rather than a three-time rhythm. On even easier ground, the spike of the axe simply trails in the snow. But that easier ground is not here.

Under the helmet brim my glacier-goggled eyes stay keen on the purple rope flicking and twisting bright against the snow ahead. I try to keep it taut enough to prevent it catching in Colin's crampons; loose enough to prevent irritating tugs on his harness. Plant, one, two. Plant, one, two. I rarely look ahead, only to discourage myself with false summits.

'The Finsteraarhorn,' I think again. 'I'm climbing it.'

First sun slinks over the saddle to our side of the mountain, and up ahead Colin's red and yellow fleece roars into a blaze. The babbling line of Italians approach behind us as we pause for photos.

'I have three young men, very strong,' their leader says to us, coming level. 'I think they can go ahead now.'

The string of three march past us, silenced by effort, carving a serpentine way around final crevasses towards the golden-glossed snow scoop of the Hugisatell. As I look towards the rock ridge to its right, a gilded line flashes up against blue sky, holds briefly and then dies over our side of the ridge – a tight whirlpool of illuminated spindrift, suggesting that our relative warmth and shelter may be short-lived once out from the lee of the mountain.

We arrive on the corniced brink where the mountain-side falls away at our feet, throwing up ahead of us all the peaks previously hidden to the east. A gnarled head of ice and rock spars up to our right where we will go next.

I learnt at the Hut that Gertrude Bell, famous as an Arabist, had made the first attempt on the north-east ridge of Finsteraarhorn in 1902. She rarely makes an appearance amongst the lists of men in Alpine climbing histories but her account of the ordeal in a letter to her father is terrifying in its detail.

'The arête… rises from the glacier in a great series of gendarmes and towers, set at such an angle on the steep face of the mountain that you wonder how they can stand at all.' Her party climbed onto the arête, 'beyond the reach of the stones the mountain had fired at us (fortunately with rather a bad aim)…', but were eventually forced to retreat, from a position within view of the summit, with 'snow blowing down the couloir in a small avalanche'.

The descent was as dangerous as the failed ascent. Amidst blizzard and mist, her ice axe was teased by lightning, which provoked her cool words: 'It's not nice to carry a private lightning conductor in your hand in the thick of a thunderstorm'. She spent the night in a tiny crack with a guide sitting on her feet to keep them warm, and continued back down the arête the next day, shivering in continuous snowfall but resolute: '… when things are as bad as ever they can be you cease to mind them much. You set your teeth and battle with the fates.'

Having reached the relative safety of the Unteraar Glacier, damp matches failed to ignite, even under the tent of her skirts, and they were forced to spend another night out, huddled against the elements, making the full expedition 57 hours. Her climbing partners later applauded her courage and endurance and her reminders to keep eating. On safe arrival at Meiringen, she consumed a great many boiled eggs and jugs of hot milk and discovered her toes to be frostbitten. This made Finsteraarhorn the last cry of her extraordinary climbing career.

In the same letter she wrote of, 'the wonderful and terrible things that happen in high places'. Perhaps it's this dichotomy of elation and terror that draws us to the knife-edge, but also what keeps people away.

I'm puzzled by the lack of women participating in such adventures today. A rough head-count at the huts revealed one woman in ten, a proportion represented in the Italian party now stamping their feet next to us. Maybe it's that women look for more meditative experiences in the mountains; suffer less summit fixation. My introduction to Alpine climbing the previous week certainly had me wondering if summit fever was for me.

There was something absurd in the convergence of scant-breathed people on coffee-table sized summits, when great sweeps of undulating ridge, glacier and col remained spread around us, pristine and unoccupied. It brought to mind John Ruskin's scathing attack on climbers and tourists despoiling the Alps in his lecture 'Sesame and Lilies' of 1864: 'The Alps themselves, which your own poets used to love so reverently, you look upon as soaped poles in a bear-garden, which you set yourselves to climb, and slide down again, with "shrieks of delight"'.

On the bus up the Val d'Hérens towards Arolla at the beginning of the trip, I'd looked longingly at green meadows, the dark weathered wood of the ship-strong houses, verges effervescing with flowers as they fell behind us. I'd had my head in a hay meadow near one of our campsites, and a cricket had whirred the clover and grass into a thrill of life. All the long walk up to the monochrome heights of Cabane de Dix, marmots whistled us through the valleys and we named the small yellow fields of pasque flowers, the quintessentially alpine gentian, alpine clover, huge bright violets.

Is this alpinism really 'me', I wondered? Don't I prefer the lower ways and passes where lives still linger, where green things grow; not these heights which above 3,000 metres seem equally to belong to any goretex-armoured warrior who gets there first? If this is Alpinism, am I really equipped to deal with its fearful implications? I began to think that the pull to the summits must be a young person's thing, that my father never had the chance to outgrow.

On one of our rest days between Arolla and the Bernese Oberland we'd met a woman who told us two climbers had been 'lost' from Cabane de Dix, just after we left. Sitting in valley sunshine about to eat fresh apricots and cinnamon buns, I'd been quite stunned by this news, as if their lives had brushed against ours before they died. I imagined being at the hut when guides brought the bodies down, the sobering of the mood, and the arrival of a sudden starker sense of danger.

I wondered why Effie Pendleton joined my father's party in 1952. The only woman. Was it to prove that she could, out of a love of high places, or simply to be in the mountains with her fiancé? I like the look of her from the one photo in which she faces the camera – a compact body that looks strong, balanced; layers of clothing peeled back for exertion; a high bounce of short dark hair, and under her goggles, an easy smile. Her hands pause in dark mittens at her sides. She looks comfortable in this environment, ready for adventure.

I've studied the guide book and know the words almost by heart, clinging to the ones that imply easiness – the

grade, *'facile'*; 'scramble' rather than 'climb'. I know that the route first traverses the western flank and then moves onto the ridge itself. Way up above us, I see the snow crests and cornices leading up the ridge until blunt rock thrusts skywards in greasy-looking blocks. No-one has been up it since this fall of snow, and it's whiter now than any of the photos I've seen.

Illuminated snowflakes float between me and the bright jackets and smiling faces of the re-assembled Italian party. They continue to stamp their feet, and have put on their windproof layers. We put on ours, re-coil the rope around our shoulders, eat chocolate. I start to feel cold. Someone has to go first.

At 9 a.m., a little more than four hours above the hut, amongst peaks in three countries stretching up to kiss the sky, and with the Italians continuing to prevaricate, we lead on.

To reach the ridge requires an awkward haul up a short, snow-silled crag. Colin pulls himself up, and fixes a belay to secure my ascent. My crampons are insecure and slippy on rock, arms too weak for the necessary push-up. The longer I flounder, the louder rises the chorus from the Italian audience behind me. Then I'm up, quickly followed by Rick, and we're moving on the loose, un-marked snow that's accumulated on the slope.

Each step is hard-earned. Colin slashes the adze of his

axe into snow until he connects with something hard – rock, older snow, ice – to which crampons will cling. Before I stretch a foot up to each step, I empty it again of the soft showerings that Colin's next cutting has sent down. I spear my pick as hard as possible into the slope to my left, seeking purchase in ice or around a rock so that a secure foothold is backed up by a hand-rail. The glove on the axe is sucked deep into soft snow, and is soon wet and freezing to the shaft.

'Remember to stand upright,' Rick calls. 'Don't hug the hill.'

And he's right. To have weight on the crampons, one needs to be perpendicular to the hill, but it feels like leaning out. I don't look down, or think of the potential slide. I look for rocks over which I can loop Rick's rope behind me, a small pivot point between us should one of us slip – probably an illusory security. I look at what's immediately ahead.

It's steep and slow, but I can breathe, my moves feel strong, and we are undoubtedly heading for the summit. A glance over my shoulder reveals the Italian hard-men, miniaturised on the Hugisatell, sitting in a sunlit pool of red coats far below, watching our progress. The glance also reveals a pair of climbers gaining on us. A beard, a pair of rectangular spectacles. New faces. We greet and agree they should pass us. Colin is tiring from all the step-cutting, and they're faster than us.

Gertrude Bell said she could recall every part of the north-east ridge, and I'm similarly gripped by the features I turn to for support, and try to trust. There is an absolute focus which knocks away any other thought, image, even a glance at the extraordinary views. There's just a faint sense of the falling away of any other land around us, our penetration into the sky, as we climb the highest in the Bernese Oberland. I barely ponder the distance to the summit, just keep an eye on the pair ahead of us, concentrate on the security of each shift in my body, the sympathy of the rope ahead to Colin.

As we move towards the crest, rock begins to burst through the snow flank. Colin points out here and there a flake to grip, something to allow the body a strong swing around an upward-jutting boulder. I know that this mountain is infamous for rock falls and that in general the risk is increasing with climate change, but I shut the thought out.

The crest is messy – jutting rock followed by corniced soft snow, a sudden shocking gulf of sky beyond it. Each step on the crest spreads a revelation of new geography; steep slopes rising in range after range below and beyond, should one dare look. We are walking in the air. Each further step is a bonus. I have no sense of time. But Colin has paused ahead.

'What are you thinking, Colin?' I ask his back.

There's a long silence. Then, 'I'm knackered.'

We can see the pair ahead have climbed up onto a prominent block, are having a drink and assessing their way ahead. There seems to be some levelling out – we can't see beyond it, and I wonder if we're nearing the summit. We pause, waiting to see what they'll do next.

'We're going to turn back,' a Czech voice calls to us.

'Yes,' says Rick behind me, as if they're confirming his own thoughts.

'There's much snow before the summit,' comes the call again. 'It will take perhaps another hour and a half. And we're concerned at the condition of the snow for the return.'

With the turn of the day, the planet, we see that the sun is now stroking the south-west face of the mountain down which we must return – warming, melting, creating hazards. An approaching tide.

None of us argue.

We move up towards the snow crest, cut a small platform on which we can perch three abreast, crampons bracing us from the drop below, so that the faster pair can pass us. Sitting close, we tame our movements to avoid dislodging each other, tease chocolate out of pockets into mouths, drink and exchange words, eyes levelling on the mountains to our west.

The Czechs begin their descent, bodies turned upright into the mountain, moving together, traversing towards us. Ice axes splutter up snow flurries, the surface a swell and fall under them. Then the men descend steeply, directly below us. I see how difficult this is going to be. Our journey is only half way complete.

I hear a bee buzz close to my ear, an incongruous reminder of the valley, hours and days below us. When will we be back again amongst flowers, crickets, bees?

'The only thing that matters,' says Rick as we set off again after the Czechs, 'is getting down safely. Take your time.' An echo of Whymper: *Do nothing in haste. Look well to each step...*

And I feel almost overwhelmed with gratitude for this permission. It calms me, and with Colin below me suggesting holds for my hands and feet, I slowly re-find the steps of our ascent, backwards. We see that the Czech climbers, having reached the Hugisatell and rejoined a third waiting there, are watching us down the steep snow flank. They get up and leave just as Colin says to me, 'You can turn outwards here', and we begin again to do something that resembles walking – become upright figures with two-time legs, arms dropping by our sides. Even the flounder-crag seems easier on descent.

Our feet touch down onto the safe-seeming, smooth snow of the Hugisatell. When we look at watches, we see that the ridge has gripped our minds and bodies for four hours. This is what Rick calls 'mental fasting', the absolute focus of mountaineering that clears all else. Now it releases us to a group hug and photos. Words flow again. We have the mountain to ourselves, and sit in a colourful row, laughing, spreading slabs of bread onto the 'table' of Rick's knees to layer with cheese and squirt with mayonnaise from a tube. We revel in a sense of achievement, but mostly just in the joy of being up here with, 'one crowded hour of glorious life,' as Whymper (quoting Walter Scott) would have it on finally reaching the summit of the Matterhorn.

Colin points north west. 'The Eiger!'

We look along the continuation of the ridge we're on. Beyond the conical white peak of the Aggasizhorn where my father stood to take photographs of Finsteraarhorn, we see the dark grey flat-topped mountain that Colin has picked out.

We spin through 360 degrees. Colin and Rick name the peaks that years of familiarity with geography, shape, and distance have made theirs. In most areas of Scotland I can do this – know hills from different angles by their relation to each other and to lochs and valleys, despite their shape-shifting. Here I'm still lost, although the characteristic shapes of the Matterhorn and Mont Blanc have followed us around enough now to be landmarks.

The dark rift of the snowless Rhone Valley separates us from the further reaches of the Valais and last week's mountains, now looking remote and white.

'How many days do you get like this in a lifetime?' asks Colin. 'Perhaps thirty? If you're lucky.'

I've walked alone so much that it strikes me suddenly this sharing is what mountaineering is about. I feel incredibly lucky to have walked the last days fastened in trust to these two men, while following my father's footsteps.

Perhaps it's this that overcomes all the absurdities of what we're doing – that mountaineering, going to the heights, keeps us young in spirit. And, as Whymper said of his scrambles in the Alps, he was repaid for his toil by two of the best things a man can have – 'health and friends'.

A bee settles next to my hand on the snow, buzzing, bright and fuzzy with heat; the valley calling.

Four hours is half an office day, a long match at Wimbledon, a short night's sleep. How had it seemed like half an hour we were on the ridge? This landscape of ice and rock seems to have exposed the elasticity of time, contracting it in some odd way relative to the primeval heartbeat of the mountains and their slow-moving glaciers.

My father, because he was just that, has always

seemed older than me. Yet he came here at half my age. The postcard he sent to his parents shows Finsteraarhorn, sharp-spiked, seen from Grindelwald. But it carries a wretched rather than a triumphant message:

'11th August 1952   Gasthof Restaurant Glacier
                                              Grindelwald

to Mr and Mrs Cracknell,
11 Earl Richard's Road North,
Exeter, Devon, Angleterre

'Dear Mum and Dad,

I am very cross that you have been told about this miserable business before I have had a chance to let you know myself… I have just got down from showing the guides where the body lay… This is what happened. We had almost finished our journey, we were roped and traversing a difficult ice fall to one side & we stopped to put on crampons to cross a steep ice slope. Three were together on a small rock and I at the back on the mass of the rock. Suddenly I saw a large boulder falling clear of the slope and shouted. The girl

was standing and did not duck quick enough
and the back of her head was smashed and
she died at once. Jim panicked & David was
personally concerned so I got them out of the
way, removed rope & gear from her and
secured her to an ice axe and then led them
off over difficult and dangerous ice to the
hut, arriving after dark. I volunteered to stay
for the guides. I look forward to home. Tell
Jenny in case papers garble.

Love Richard'.

In an extra note he added: 'incident at very top left of
photo'. I've studied the picture on the postcard again and
again. His description suggests the near vertical eastern
side of the ridge. I tried to convince myself before the
climb that it must be a trick of perspective, re-reading his
note to try and find a different meaning, a different
location from that high, haunting spear of mountain. I'm
still puzzled how his party came to be so high up so late
in the day. But none of that matters now, and it seems
there is no-one left to tell me.

    In the same photo album, amongst the postcards and
photos, is fastened the reason for the family memory of
the mountain's name, a small stark press clipping:

'STONE KILLS A GIRL CLIMBER
10,000 ft Up Mountain

Grindelwald, Bernese Oberland, Sunday – Mountain guides today carried down Miss Effie Pendleton, 24, an Oxford student killed by a falling stone 10,000ft up the Finsteraarhorn. – Reuter.'

I wonder if it came to haunt him – this place, the 'miserable business' that befell him here. Gertrude Bell pokes two fingers in my ribs – one for 'terrible', one for 'wonderful', for they are both here with my father and myself, juxtaposed. I wonder if my joy now can mend that dark twist in history.

This mammoth ridge that towers over and arcs through the Bernese Oberland, must have represented my father's threshold into adulthood. As he descended the mountain for the second time, with guides carrying Effie Pendleton's body, he was setting out on a longer journey, well beyond the mountain hut – to the green valleys, to Exeter and parents, to Middlesbrough to take up his first job as an industrial chemist for ICI making the pink plastic 'gums' into which false teeth are fixed. He would be engaged to my mother in less than six months, married and starting a family by 1954. Finsteraarhorn was his last venture into high places.

He and my mother moved to the Netherlands with my brother and sister for his job with Royal Dutch/Shell in 1958, where I was born the following year. From there we took family holidays in the green van with a square ventilator in the roof that's one of my earliest memories. On reaching the Austrian Alps, we no doubt kept him low in the valleys, and I imagine him throwing occasional glances to the snow-peaks, and thinking of a time, when we were older, when he might climb again, and perhaps introduce us to the high places.

Rick is beginning to do this with his fearless eight year old son. I imagine them coming to the Alps soon, a garrulous pair, with matching smiles and long legs and their affinity for rock and heights. The manager of the mountain shop in Fiesch told us that it would soon be the fiftieth anniversary of his first ascent of Finsteraarhorn, made at eight years of age with his father. Such markers of the years, celebrations of age and youth pulse though family memory. My father had all that to look forward to as I weighed on his back in the Austrian Alps, a wordless cargo. Apparently he carried me to the edge of a glacier, just to see it, and to marvel.

I think of the slow digging of a platform in the snow, the necessary anchoring of the body, and the marking of the spot. A distraught fiancé to bring to safety. How quickly my father must have had to grow up. The youthful alpine-aired faces in the photos from Arolla just two weeks before, turn away from the camera towards serious responsibilities, jobs and death.

As we revel on the Hugisatell, the only reliable thing about time seems to be the point in the day's turning – the sun is full on our route down and branding the skin of our exposed faces with reflected fire.

We descend the long, slushy slope to the hut, playfully when it allows – a glissading, rope-tugged bum slide – and seriously when sun-softened snow bridges have to be negotiated over crevasses. My face throbs where the insistent running of my nose has allowed the sun to pierce Factor 40 cream. Fiescherhorn and Gross Grün-horn grow higher and spikier ahead of us, polarised black and white as we sink lower. The unpredictable terrain of previous steps retrodden and shuffled into a mess of hard and soft now undermines our balance. I am unstable and lurching, rhythm-less, tugging taut the rope. Massive snow balls form on the base of my crampons and I jig along to my newly learnt tap dance with the ice axe dislodging them at each alternate step.

We gain rock above the hut with relief, un-pincer feet from crampons, cast off the rope to make ourselves independent people again, turn our faces at last away from the scouring heat. We scramble down the rocks that were in darkness when we came up at dawn. My legs still feel surprisingly strong and sure. Our return is heralded by the scavenging choughs.

Twelve hours after our departure we find the Hut transformed. The flags hang limp, the storm-swept wooden deck is now lined with drying boots and climbing gear. Dozens of T-shirted people brought from all directions by fine weather and firming snow are bathing in the afternoon glacier-light which we quickly retreat from, indoors. Amongst the buzz of beer drinking, the anticipation for many of the next day's climb, the Italian group is diminished by the new throng. They applaud our return. We catch at the eyes of two faces that feature a beard and a pair of rectangular spectacles and then burst into smiles. We drink a litre of sweet tea each and apple juice, too high to feel tired or sunburnt or sore-legged.

'I'm looking forward to seeing a tree,' says Colin, as if each day of our exile in this enchanted black and white world has been a year.

None of the three of us seems to feel that we failed to climb the mountain.

The next day we return over the Grünhornlücke Pass. The slim, pioneer trail we made two days earlier has now been broadened by successive parties. Where we had been presented by a wall of fog on our journey here, we now turn to see the full west face of the Finsteraarhorn.

High above the Frühstückplatz, where the climbable slope rises under the sheer face of the summit ridge, the wisdom of our decision to turn back has been spelt out. A chaotic scribble of avalanched snow now partially covers the curved line of our footprints. We pause for a long while in the morning sun while we contemplate this.

Two strings of climbers appear from the direction of Konkordiaplatz to our west, their faces kissed into smiles by the levelling ground and sudden rise of Finsteraarhorn ahead of them. Rather as I imagine might happen in a chance meeting of hunters, they seek out our experience, asking about directions and conditions; part as colleague, part competitor. Then they move on, summit-hungry.

Unroping, we step out onto the slow deep sea of the Konkordiaplatz, the junction of streams of time. An eight hundred metre depth of ice moves in invisible increments under our feet. Like a tree and its rings, or a cross-section of coral that reveals growth bands through centuries, the glacier archives events of weather, and perhaps of human travel.

A little removed by the creep of the glacier lies my father's way across here. I wonder how far downstream the imprints of his feet have drifted in 56 years, try to imagine their changed patina, perhaps transformed into something resembling a fossilised leaf.

Whilst standing on this great sweep of a meeting place, my mobile phone signal returns for the first time in two days. I send home a message of reassurance; history has not repeated itself like the crossing of a dark rope.

I am warmed by midday sun, the Aletsch glacier is rumbling and gurgling off into the far distance ready to carry us downhill. In a matter of weeks the superficial imprints of the journey – bruised shins, sunburnt lips – will have healed. But I know this experience will echo on. A spell has been untied; a story retraced and given words out of silence.

Postscript: September '08

A reply comes from The Alpine Club in London. My father was never a member. But they do have a press clipping about the accident which I haven't yet seen. They have kindly sent it on.

I read:

'WOMAN STUDENT KILLED
Geneva, Aug 10

Four English Alpinists climbing to the Finster-aarjoch (10,925 ft) on Friday were making for the Strahlegg Hut (8,858 ft) when they were overtaken by an avalanche of stones. One, Miss E R Pendle-ton, of Oxford, a student, was struck and killed. The others, who were unhurt, went for help. A party of eight guides from Grindelwald made an eight-hour ascent to recover the body, which late last night was brought down to the village.'

I look again at the map to try and make sense of this additional detail of geography. The Finsteraarjoch is north-east of the summit of Agassizhorn; the Strahlegg Hut further north-east still. This implies they were descending when the accident happened, and not descending from Finsteraarhorn but from Agassizhorn. 'Our journey was nearly over', suddenly makes more sense. They were heading for the valley, on their way to Grindelwald in the north-east. I look again at the postcard: 'incident at very top left of photo'. Below the high sharp spear of the iconic mountain I see for the first time a lower lump, further left. It would have been on their descent route. I am swept to a new conclusion.

My father clearly admired Finsteraarhorn, but didn't climb it. He chose instead a pleasing south-west to north-east traverse that probably took four or five days across the entire dramatic sweep of the Bernese Oberland, denying the enigmatic tug of its highest peak except as a sight along the way.

I'd been distracted by the spear of mountain and overlooked its lower foothills; saw my father as forever-youthful, striving for the highest summits. In this way, his memory beguiled me into a climb far more challenging than I would have chosen myself. After my initial dismay at 'doing the wrong mountain', I've come to see it as his joke on me.

I also see how unreliable memory is, and how buried it becomes. My detective trails were slow and mazed, but it makes sense now that it was on Konkordiaplatz, rather than on the high mountain, that I felt the deep pull of our affinity; our common journeys. Somewhere on the slow glacier the plates of ice we've each trodden ground against each other, and our paths coincided.

Bibliography

Travels with a Donkey in the Cévennes, Robert Louis
    Stevenson, 1879
Another Man's Shoes, Sven Sømme, Polperro Heritage
    Press, 2005
Yuli Somme Felt Maker: www.yulisomme.co.uk
Norway's Resistance Museum: www.forsvaretsmuseer.no/
    nor/Hjemmefrontmuseet/Om-museet
Modern Painters, Part V Mountain Beauty, John Ruskin,
    1856
Scrambles Amongst the Alps 1860-1869, Edward Whymper,
    National Geographic Adventure Classics, 2002
Letters of Gertrude Bell Vol I, Ernest Benn Ltd, 1927
Finsteraarhorn: Die Einsame Spitze, Daniel Anker (editor),
    AS Verlag & Buchkonzept, 1997
Mountains of the Mind, Robert Macfarlane, Granta, 2003

Acknowledgements

Sincere thanks to the Sømme family both in Britain and Norway for involving me in Sven's journey with such openness and warmth, and to our many Norwegian hosts and contacts who brought the story alive with their memories as well as helping us in practical ways. Special thanks to Ellie and Yuli for their determination and companionship. Thanks also to Ellie and to Polperro Heritage Press for permission to quote from Sven's own account, now republished as *Another Man's Shoes*.

To my brave and good-humoured climbing partners in the Alps, Rick Worrell and Colin Hughes, I owe a huge debt. I'm also indebted to the people who helped fill in my Father's life and adventures including Andrew Ross, ex-President of the Oxford University Mountaineering Club, Marian Dawson, Anne Colman, my uncle Martin Cracknell and mother Jenny Scanlan.

Thanks for permission to use photos taken by Colin Hughes, Rick Worrell and Yuli Sømme and for use of photos belonging to the Sømme family and the Municipal Archives of Trondheim.

I'm grateful to Kit Shepherd for his expert editorial

input and to 'eagle-eye' Ruary Mackenzie Dodds for proof-reading.

ALBA | CHRUTHACHAIL

The writing of *Following our Fathers* and a number of other walking stories was made possible by a Creative Scotland Award in 2007.

About the Author

Linda Cracknell's short fiction has been published in two collections: *Life Drawing* (2000) and *The Searching Glance* (2008). She also writes drama for BBC Radio 4, and is editor of a non-fiction anthology on the wild places of Britain and Ireland, *A Wilder Vein* (2009). She regularly takes walks with a pen in hand in pursuit of stories. The full collection which the two essays published here belong to – *Doubling Back* – was shortlisted for the Robin Jenkins Literary Award in 2009 and is unpublished at the time of this volume going to print.

Other titles from 'best foot books'

WHITER THAN WHITE
A story of footsteps, suds and secrets on the Isle of Rum in 1913. 2009, ISBN 978-0-9562453-0-4, £4

THE BEAT OF HEART STONES
A walker falls into step with a dry stone dyke on Schiehallion and hears its story. 2010, ISBN 978-0-9562453-1-1, £4

Available from: www.lindacracknell.com